# SUMMARY

## Principles - Life and Work

### by Ray Dalio

Essential Insight Summaries

© **Copyright 2019 by Essential Insight Summaries**

**All rights reserved.**

This document is geared toward providing exact and reliable information with regard to the topic and issue covered. The publication is sold with the idea that the publisher is not required to render accounting, officially permitted, or otherwise, qualified services. If advice is necessary, legal or professional, a practiced individual in the profession should be ordered.

In no way is it legal to reproduce, duplicate, or transmit any part of this document in either electronic means or in printed format. Recording of this publication is strictly prohibited and any storage of this document is not allowed unless with written permission from the publisher. All rights reserved.

The information provided herein is stated to be truthful and consistent, in that any liability, in terms of inattention or otherwise, by any usage or abuse of any policies, processes, or directions contained within is the solitary and utter responsibility of the recipient reader. Under no circumstances will any legal responsibility or blame be held against the publisher for any reparation, damages, or monetary loss due to the information herein, either directly or indirectly.

Respective authors own all copyrights not held by the publisher.

The information herein is offered for informational purposes solely, and is universal as so. The presentation of the information is without contract or any type of guarantee assurance.

The trademarks that are used are without any consent, and the publication of the trademark is without permission or backing by the trademark owner. All trademarks and brands within this book are for clarifying purposes only and are owned by the owners themselves, not affiliated with this document.

ISBN: **9781097828357**

# TABLE OF CONTENTS

**BOOK ABSTRACT**..................................................................5
**ABOUT THE AUTHOR**..........................................................7
**IMPORTANT NOTE ABOUT THIS BOOK**............................9
**PART I: WHERE RAY DALIO IS COMING FROM**...............10
**PART II: LIFE PRINCIPLES**................................................17
Chapter 1: Embrace Reality and Deal with It............................18
Chapter 2: Use the 5-Step Process to Get What You Want Out of Life........................................................................................22
Chapter 3: Be Radically Open-Minded.....................................26
Chapter 4: Understand That People Are Wired Very Differently...29
Chapter 5: Learn How to Make Decisions Effectively.............32
**PART III: WORK PRINCIPLES**...........................................34
**TO GET THE CULTURE RIGHT…**.....................................37
Chapter 1: Trust in Radical Truth and Radical Transparency...........37
Chapter 2: Cultivate Meaningful Work and Meaningful Relationships.............................................................................40
Chapter 3: Create a Culture in Which it is Okay to Make Mistakes And Unacceptable Not to Learn from Them............43
Chapter 4: Get and Stay in Sync...............................................46
Chapter 5: Believability Weight Your Decision Making.........50
Chapter 6: Recognize How to Get Beyond Disagreements.....54
**TO GET THE PEOPLE RIGHT…**........................................57
Chapter 7: Remember That the WHO Is More Important Than the WHAT...........................................................................57
Chapter 8: Hire Right, Because the Penalties for Hiring Wrong Are Huge....................................................................................60
Chapter 9: Constantly Train, Test, Evaluate, and Sort People......63
**TO BUILD AND EVOLVE YOUR MACHINE**.....................66
Chapter 10: Manage as Someone Operating a Machine to Achieve a Goal..........................................................................66
Chapter 11: Perceive and Don't Tolerate Problems.................70
Chapter 12: Diagnose Problems to Get at Their Root Causes......72

Chapter 13: Design Improvements to Your Machine
to Get Around Your Problems................................................................75
Chapter 14: Do What You Set Out to Do...............................................79
Chapter 15: Use Tools and Protocols to Shape How Work Is Done....81
Chapter 16: And for Heaven's Sake, Don't Overlook Governance! ...83
**CONCLUSION**......................................................................................85

# BOOK ABSTRACT

Life is constantly moving and filled with activities. Human nature is geared toward attaining success in all we embark on, however; not everyone understands the way to achieve this success. This book is divided into three parts:

## Part I: Where Ray Dalio is coming from

This portion is basically centered on his life experiences. How the activities he has carried out helped shape his personal life and helped him in growing his company. Also, in this portion there is an extensive record of areas Mr. Dalio succeeded and those where things didn't exactly go according to plan.

## Part II: Life Principles

Every event that takes places in life occurs as a result of the cause-effect relationship that exists between our actions and inactions. As human beings we are not just made up of flesh and blood, but by emotions, personality, thought processes, dreams. They all play a pivotal role in our life.

The principles discussed in this segment of the book were derived from my personal experience and knowledge I have gathered over the years. The principles discussed are outlined in three levels: higher-level principle, mid-level principle, and sub-level principle.

## Part III: Work Principles

Work principles are centered on applying the life principle to an organization or work setting. For every organization to function well, the work principle must be aligned with the life principles of their members. The principles must not necessarily align on all points. When there is a synchronization between both principles, there is increased fulfillment in role execution.

These principles consist of rules for managing people and providing steps to help managers and employees function better. Concepts such as idea meritocracy, believability-weighted decision-making, radical truth, and radical transparency will be discussed in detail to show their application can lead to organization success.

## ABOUT THE AUTHOR

Ray Dalio was born in 1949 and grew up in a middle-class Long Island neighborhood. The only son of a professional jazz musician and a stay-at-home mom. He was an ordinary kid in an ordinary house and a worse-than-ordinary student. He loved playing around with his pals and was not a big fan of formalized education because he had memorizing issues.

While playing golf at Links golf club Mr. Dalio was first introduced to investment. Being twelve at that time and in love with finance, he started purchasing stocks and reading up on his own to get a better understanding of the financial world.

After several successful investments, which were guided by his limited knowledge of investing and buying stocks, he was exposed to failure and crashing markets in 1966, and all his knowledge of the financial world was finally proven wrong.

Mr. Dalio studied finance in college and created the company, "Bridgewater." The principles being shared in this book have been practiced in both his personal life and in running his organization.

We hope these principles help you as much as they have helped him in achieving success.

# IMPORTANT NOTE ABOUT THIS BOOK

At Essential Insight Summaries, we pride ourselves in providing key points in life-changing books in the shortest amount of time. Our summaries focus on bringing vital information that enhances your knowledge and understanding, in a specific subject matter. We focus on the essentials, to ensure you maximize knowledge in the shortest possible time.

This comprehensive summary is based on *Principles: Life and Work* by Ray Dalio and does not share any affiliation with the author or original work in any way or form. The summary does not utilize any text from the original work. We want our readers to use this summary as a study companion to the original book, and not as a substitute.

# PART I

# WHERE RAY DALIO IS COMING FROM

"Time is like a river that carries us forward into encounters with reality that require us to make decisions. We can't stop our movement down this river, and we can't avoid those encounters. We can only approach them in the best possible way."

Growing up, we are shaped both by our DNA and our environment. For Mr. Dalio, his obvious weakness was bad rote memory, which resulted in him hating school.

John F. Kennedy was an intelligent, charismatic man who painted vivid pictures of changing the world for the better by achieving equal rights and eliminating poverty. His ideas had a major effect on Mr. Dalio's thinking.

Mr. Dalio majored in finance during college because of his love for the market and because that field had no foreign language requirement, which gave him the opportunity to learn both inside and outside classroom.

In 1966, asset prices reflected investors' optimism about the future, but between 1967 and 1979, bad economic surprises led to big and unexpected price declines; every sector of America felt it. The economy and the markets were the worse hit areas.

While at Harvard Business school (HBS), Mr. Dalio begged for a summer job to trade commodities at Merrill Lynch. During that period, people from Harvard were mainly focused on trading stocks. This role prepared him for his job at Dominick & Dominick, as a commodities manger. However, this duty did not last long because the company was taken down soon after the stock market crashed. He moved on to bigger, more successful brokerage firms.

Just after he graduated from HBS and went to work in commodities at Dominick & Dominick, Mr. Dalio set up a little business with Bob Scott, a friend from HBS, along with a few friends in other countries. The company was focused on trading commodities. By 1975, he restarted the company with its original name of Bridgewater. After investing in stocks and commodities, he ventured into livestock, meat, grain, and oilseed markets because they were more concrete. In the agricultural world, he created his own logical design with emphasis on cause-effect relationships.

From 1950 until 1980, debt, inflation, and growth moved up and down in constant larger waves, with each bigger than the one before. In August 1982, Mexico defaulted on its debt and Mr. Dalio was sure that other countries would follow suit in defaulting. He was dead wrong.

In response to this event, the federal reserve made money more readily available and this caused the stock market to jump by a record amount, leading to a drop in inflation and a sporadic growth in the economy. Mr. Dalio lost so much money because of his earlier prediction, which led him to buying gold and T-bill futures as a spread against Eurodollars. Eventually he had to let all his workers go at Bridgewater and was faced with a tough decision of starting again or quitting.

He sought out the opinion of people who did not agree with his choices and reviewed their points with an open-mind.

Coming out of his crash, Mr. Dalio was so broke he couldn't muster enough money to pay for an airplane ticket to Texas to visit a prospective client. He did keep working and started rebuilding his team from ground zero.

His first investment after returning was to buy computers because they helped him process large amounts of data. Sometimes, he jokingly said, *"He might to have become successful without them because the computer was much better than his brain in "thinking" about many things at once."*

By late 1983, even though he had just six employees, Mr. Dalio created a system that ensured there were checks and balance in making decisions for Bridgewater.

By the mid-1980s, Bridgewater was making good calls on interest rates and currency markets. The institutional investment managers who were buying their research were using it to make money and they were successfully managing companies' interest rates and currency exposures. These factors were the turning point for the company.

As the 1990's rolled in, Bridgewater was in a comfortable position and exceeding expectations as one of the few organizations that made profit, especially after what they had gone through in October 1988, known as "Black Friday."

The company continued to make mistakes, though they were all within their range of expectations. Mr. Dalio created an operating system that helped his staff evaluate him without the fear of criticism, and by 1995, Bridgewater had grown to forty-two employees and $4.1 billion in investments.

Under management, things were not so much different. He ensured the company ran on a transparency policy that allowed everyone to be involved and be accountable. By 2000, this figure multiplied, and Bridgewater was now handling over 32 billion in investments.

With the rapid growth the company was experiencing, Mr. Dalio created principles and guidelines to ensure everyone was united, even in their different roles.

In 2006, Mr. Dalio prepared a rough list of approximately sixty Work Principles and distributed them to Bridgewater's managers so they could begin to evaluate them, debate them, and make sense of them for themselves. This idea he created led to the beginning of an evolutionary process in the company.

By 2010, Mr. Dalio was already concerned about transitioning out of his roles in Bridgewater as CEO and CIO; jobs which were critical to the existence of the company. As the company turned forty in 2015, Mr. Dalio recounts that while the principles of operating had stayed, they had evolved over time.

Their culture of striving for excellence in work and excellence in relationships by being radically truthful and radically transparent with each other remained the same. He recounted how they uniquely and repeatedly tried new things, failed, learned from their failures, improved, and tried again, doing that over and over in an upward spiral to ensure that success was sustained.

# PART II

## LIFE PRINCIPLES

# CHAPTER 1

## EMBRACE REALITY AND DEAL WITH IT

Success requires an understanding of life, how life really works, and how to deal with it to achieve the best possible outcome in any given situation. However, the mindset it individually brings to the table in handling these issues might be the defining factor between attaining success or losing in this game of life.

In order to live a successful life, there must be a combination of our dreams, unwavering determination, and an accurate understanding of reality. Without these, the possibility of attaining great success appears bleak. In life, change is constant. This change, when used as a projectile to attain success, comes by unlearning and relearning concepts.

Even evolution shows us that these concepts are the keys to continuous survival. Radically open-minded nature and radical transparency accelerates learning. Fear is innate to man. However, to conquer this innate barrier, we need to learn how to be radically open-minded and truthful in all aspects of our lives because eventually they bring forth changing relationships, both with our peers and superiors as the case may be.

Humans are considered as higher animals because of our brain's ability to process information from a higher level of understanding. This is our "singular most distinctive quality."

To understand how reality operates, we must look at life from two perspectives: "top down and bottom up." Top down viewing of problems, allows us to interpret them from the point of natural laws and is a better way to handle delicate life situations. For the world to recognize and appreciate your ideas. The solutions provided must be in synchronization with the laws governing reality and evolution. As fear is innate to man, so, also, is survival.

Evolution and history has shown us that there will always be rewards for consistent advancement of one's goals. In an organizational setting, everyone's goals should be one and the same with the group's goal and vision. The understanding that we are both everything and nothing when we look at ourselves from our point of view and the universe's point of view will eventually determine what we evolve into.

According to famous psychologist Sigmund Freud: "Love and work are the cornerstone of our humanness." To harness our skills and talent to achieve the best possible results. Pain, gains, and constant examination of whatever position we are in, are two sides of the coin called progress we must deal with. Avoiding the pain would put us in a comfortable position but this position would not give us the level of progress required for great success.

Every choice made comes with three sets of consequences. Our ability to view each consequence-order objectively and overcome the temptations to view our decisions in one order of consequences alone would most likely translate to having a successful life. No matter the circumstance our actions or inactions produces, we should accept responsibility for them.

Life goals can be compared to machines. They are designed and manufactured with components that ensure they function appropriately. The design process is crucial but without the manufacturing process, our goals would never the executed. By comparing or contrasting and knowing how exactly you fit into your goals, the expected outcomes of the goal can be modified and redesigned to ensure better results are produced.

At times when you cannot objectively view your goals or determine how exactly you fit into them, it is essential to seek the help of a higher qualified person to maintain objectivity.

## CHAPTER 2

## USE THE 5-STEP PROCESS TO GET WHAT YOU WANT OUT OF LIFE

Evolution, which leads to human survival both in terms of our biology and life process takes place in five distinct processes.

In unison, these steps form a loop that should be carried out one at a time as well as in sequence. It is almost near impossible to carry out these processes without making mistakes, but it is relevant for you to see them as what they are: "mistakes," learn from them and move on.

**Step 1**: Have distinct and ambiguity-free aspirations.

An African proverb says, "All things can be done, but not all things are essential to be done." This phrase describes the need to prioritize in the pursuing of our goals and ambitions. Very often, our desires are first-order consequences of our decisions. To attain the best possible result, you would need to move to the second and third level consequence to carry out actions that would ultimately lead to the fulfillment of your goals. After the creation of a clear goal, learning how to handle setbacks that would pop up along the way, being flexible, and accountable are just as important as making progress.

**Step 2**: Identify and don't tolerate problems.

Earlier on we established that pain is inevitable in making good progress. In this step, it is mandatory we identify every loophole in our plans. Similarly, we showed that man is naturally scared of painful situations. Today, to succeed in this world of over 7-billion, an individual's ability to transform pain into a learning situation is the edge needed for rapid success. It is important we note that acknowledging and surrendering to weaknesses are two different events. Time should be invested in solving the real problem rather than the cause thereof. In order to succeed, a fierce intolerance for loopholes should be developed.

**Step 3**: After loopholes are discovered in execution of our goals.

Strategic thinking is necessary to identify and differentiate between the root cause and proximate causes of a problem. Recognizing the nature possessed by an individual would help differentiate between people who would help you attain your goals and those who will pull you down.

**Step 4**: Design a plan.

There exists more than one path to achieve every goal in existence; it is either you don't know that path or are unwilling to take it. Imagine that every problem you face occurs as a result of the goal design and execution method you take. Time is of the essence in designing great plans. This does not mean that good plans cannot be created in a short period of time. Remember: "designing precedes doing."

**Step 5**: History has shown us that plans and new problems will arise and always be solved.

Evolution has demonstrated that solutions that evolve continuously to meet the current situation and demand eventually live on. Create your plans and pursue them to fulfillment. Note: To remain relevant, evolution is essential and weaknesses would make no significant difference as long solutions are found.

## CHAPTER 3

## BE RADICALLY OPEN-MINDED

The importance of a radical open-minded nature cannot be overemphasized. This factor is single-handedly the most important attribute needed for immense success. Human existence, as we know it, has always been governed by decision-making. There are two fatal flaws that create barriers in the process of making good choices.

These flaws are an individual's ego and blind spot. Ego here is referring to our subliminal inbuilt defense system that resides in the primitive area of our brain. As a result, everyone possesses two level of themselves; the higher level and lower level self, which are continuously at war with each other.

Radical open-mindedness is the ability to realize there are different point of views to every situation as well as view every situation objectively without letting your ego or blind spot mar the decision process. Open-mindedness goes way beyond knowing your point of view might not be correct. It involves other factors such as: asking the right questions from people who are more knowledgeable on the topic, getting all relevant information needed to arrive at a decision, realize that it is more important to learn and gain perspective than making judgement, out-sourcing for answers might be the way forward, and finally, be aware of your surroundings; knowing when to argue and when to seek information.

Solutions do not only come from agreements, they also come from thoughtful disagreements. In this process, the goal is to discover which point of view is correct rather than be assertive about your point of view. To determine the correct decision, opinions can be obtained from different experts. Close-minded people possess some qualities such as: are more interested in being correct than learning, are less likely to ask questions from others, prevent others from sharing their views, lack a deep sense humility, which can be noticed in the way they address issues. These qualities are important when forming relationships and aligning oneself with decision-makers.

Good news! It doesn't matter if you are close-minded naturally, open mindedness can be learned. The first step toward open-mindedness is to understand the signs of close-mindedness. Next is the identification of your blind spots; this step is crucial in attaining objectivity, get the opinion of well-informed and believable people. Meditation is another way to achieve open-mindedness, although this step can be skipped since it is not essential. Use evidence in making decisions, and finally, know when to stop seeking other options and follow through with the options available to use.

CHAPTER 4

## UNDERSTAND THAT PEOPLE ARE WIRED VERY DIFFERENTLY

The human brain is so complex that a group of individuals might be experiencing the same event at the same time but would be processing them differently.

Not every difference is bad. In fact, some differences are very good as they allow for a variety of ways to interpret a situation. The physiological composition of our brains plays a huge role determining, in most situations, how we respond to situations and events presented before us. Chemicals, such as serotonin and dopamine play a huge role in determining our physical mode, which can result in our state of mind most of the time. In essence, we are born with attributes that can both hurt us or help us, depending on how we harness them.

We established earlier that our brain's genetic components could make or mar us. The same applies to our work and relationships. Scientifically, it has been established that a brain is programmed to seek pleasure and avoid pain. Leonard Mlodinow stated in one of his books that the human social IQ is the distinguishing attribute possessed by humans. This skill has ensured that man has survived over the years and evolved into homo sapiens as we know today. In the work place, groups harmonized in their goals are more powerful than individuals when working together. An organization's culture determines which function workers align with.

The human brain has two distinct sections: conscious and subconscious mind. Neurophysiologists believe these parts are responsible for our thinking and emotions. The conscious mind can be addressed as the higher-level while the subconscious mind can be called the lower-level you. Over time, great discoveries often pop up from our subconscious.

The greatest battles faced by man is the one fought between following the direction of his feeling or thoughts. For most people, these battle never ends. However, in order to attain great success, everyone should be able to reconcile their feelings and thoughts. Habits are activities we continuously repeat; they put our brain on auto-pilot. Every man must strive to acquire good habits so as to improve their path toward achieving success. The lower-level, you are emotional and carry out activities embedded in your genes. To rewrite this program, we must build the right habits through patience and continuous practice.

Biases wired into us makes our self-assessment highly incorrect. However, through empirical psychological testing we discover that humans have several different characteristics. For example, some people are introverts while other are extroverts, some people make decisions based on logical reasoning while other hinge on their intuition, some people carry out plans and adhere to them to the letter while others are flexible and spontaneous, etc. Getting the right people to function in our lives would help us in achieving our goals in the long run.

## CHAPTER 5

## LEARN HOW TO MAKE DECISIONS EFFECTIVELY

Decision-making occurs in a two-step process: the learning and the deciding. Harmful emotions are the biggest threat to execution of goals. In learning, we are actively changing our existing knowledge but in making decisions. We are choosing how exactly we want to achieve our laid-out goals, because we are constantly faced with situations where decisions must be made. We need to ensure that our choices are not guided by every information we come across because not all of them would lead to our desired destination.

Time, they say, heals all wounds. In this context, the focus is not on healing but on approximations and the ability to achieve the best results from any given situation. This is known as the 80/20 rule. Time is spent extensively on attaining the expected perfect result in any given situation. In making progress, we need to learn to navigate between each decision and determine the best time to spend on every choice we are faced with to avoid unnecessary time wasting.

Decisions needed to achieve success needs to be consistent on all levels of occurrence because in the long-term, consistency would result in better value when success is measured.

In investment management, the principle of high risk and high return is thought on all levels of investing. This same principle resonates with making decisions. To obtain the best results from our choices, a level of risk is required to improve the expected returns. Knowing when to proceed and when to hold on could be the determiner between a high-rewarding decision and a low-rewarding decision. Ultimately, in achieving success we need to prioritize not just by the level of urgency of our choices but by comparing the odds between making a decision and not making one.

Finally, to achieve your goals, simplify the decision-making process, follow already established standards, and be cautious even when using the service of artificial intelligence. More than anything else to attain the best possible life, know the best decision and be ready to follow them with actions.

# PART III

## WORK PRINCIPLES

This segment of the principles by Ray focuses on the people working together and how to achieve the best results because groups working in harmony produce better results than individuals working alone.

Mr. Dalio stated that these work principles are basically his life principles applied to a group rather than individuals. Mr. Dalio stated, "for any group or organization to function well, its work principles must be aligned with its members' life principles."

Every organization comprises of people and a laid-out culture. These aspects do not work independently of each other, they work together to progressively continue producing results. Organizations with great work culture and environment are constantly faced with trying situations but their ability to overcome these problems and a manager's ability to accurately decipher which issues to handle and how to handle them distinguishes them from other organizations.

In life principles, we discussed radical open-mindedness but when a group is under consideration radical transparency and truth is essential to give everyone a collective stack in the group. This truth involves no sugar-coating or soft peddling of hardcore issues but rather the ability to present them as they exist. Operating in this way may seem anti-productive but as progress roles in the benefit of this method of operation becomes obvious.

# TO GET THE CULTURE RIGHT...

## CHAPTER 1

## TRUST IN RADICAL TRUTH AND RADICAL TRANSPARENCY

Success is like a bowl of salad or cooking a meal, it requires different ingredients, in different quantities, and time of addition to ensure the best result is achieved. In the work place, idea meritocracy can be practiced but only when the organization culture gives room for transparency and truth saying.

Every system is made up of supporting parts without which the whole might not function properly. Humans have flexibility to learn and unlearn by virtue of their brain power. The level of radical truth and transparency needed to achieve great success would require a level of practice to come to fruition because not all brains are wired to function on that level.

A part of the Christian holy book says, "the truth will ultimately set you free." The moment a man is considered honest and trustworthy, he has every right to demand the same treatment from everyone he encounters and interacts with. The truth should not be feared but rather should be embraced as a crucial part of winning. Workers are bound by a cord of friendship and loyalty to each other. This should in no way be placed ahead of a general loyalty to the organization they stand for.

Communication is made up of different processes but of importance. There is the creation of message by a sender and the understanding of that message by the receiver, issues should be discussed honestly and transparently until all parties involved achieves a consensus. Of great importance is the fact that we should not always assume everyone is as honest as we are, because they can affect the company's overall image. Radical transparency should not be mistaken as a pass to have no confidential or sensitive information, because this would be a huge mistake on your part. All great brands have their trade secret that gives them an edge over other competitors. Transparency can serve an organization in different ways. Justice can be achieved and accountability can be confirmed for all team members. Finally, a combination of radical truth and transparency would result in meaningful work-place relationships which would definitely translate to achievement of goals and plans.

## CHAPTER 2

## CULTIVATE MEANINGFUL WORK AND MEANINGFUL RELATIONSHIPS

Managing an organization can be both stressful and fun. Excellence can be obtained from the nature of our relationships with beneficial relationships providing an invaluable measure to help in sustaining the work place culture both for the managers and workers alike. Managers should learn that when workers are treated as more than just another part of the organization, they develop a fierce loyalty to the company and see the company's goals as theirs.

In trying to create meaningful bonds and friendships between workers, not all workers would be interested in joining this process. As long as they are loyal to the organization's mission and do not go about disrupting the smooth flow of business, they can be retained. Empathy, like every means of communication, is spoken by one person and interpreted by another.

If radical transparency and truth are practiced, being mindful of other people's feelings and wants as long as they are aligned with the organization's principle and laws can improve the work environment. However, behaviors that are clearly derogatory and offensive should not be allowed to thrive. Psychology has made us understand that incentives motivate people to work harder, but there should always be a clear distinction between generosity and fairness as they are entirely different concepts. It is good to be generous as this can act as an incentive in the work place but there should be a point where generosity stops to avoid destroying work place relationships rather than building them.

Payment and working are simultaneous activities in almost all spheres of life. When an individual provides services beyond the stipulated requirements, such person should receive a form of payment. It might be monetary or not, as this would enhance the relationship between the employers and employees. Big companies are faced with the challenge of knowing each individual worker. This factor also affects the creation of meaningful work place relationships.

In fair trade, the business person would seem to be working in your favor by giving discounts for increased number of buys made. If we take a closer look at this scenario, the trader appears to be working in your interest but is fulfilling his own mandate of making sales which shows he/she was working for their benefit not yours, as you may have assumed.

In an organization that practices decentralization of power and decision-making, every employer must pay close attention to ensure workers are working toward achieving the group goal rather than their personal goal. Although workers who succeed in developing meaningful relationships with each other take on the organization's goals as theirs, these sorts of people do not need extra supervision to perform whole-heartedly and would treat you fairly even in your absence.

## CHAPTER 3

## CREATE A CULTURE IN WHICH IT IS OKAY TO MAKE MISTAKES AND UNACCEPTABLE NOT TO LEARN FROM THEM

Mistakes. We already know they are inevitable in life. Everyone makes them. The defining factor between success and failure is the ability to learn from mistakes made. Thomas Edison once said, "I have not failed. I've just found ten thousand ways that do not work."

Pain is most likely an indication that we are moving in the right direction. Mistakes are always accompanied by the pain of their occurrence. Behind every success story is the tale of errors and mistakes. Billionaires such as Jeff Bezos, Bill Gates, etc., did not succeed without going through their own fair share of errors. It is one thing to fail on the way to achieving success, it is another thing to fail well. Failing well involves learning from errors made and taking steps to avoid making them again. In fact, mistakes should be handled like winning a tuition-free master class in your favorite course. That way, we pay attention to the details and learn better.

Everyone is faced with insecurities and fear of criticism but in truth constructive criticism is as much a valuable input and attaining success because they would help us improve our ways and increase productivity. Instead of focusing on who takes the blame or who takes the credit. In any given situation, it is better we focus on learning and translating the lessons learned to new situations in which we find ourselves.

Strategic identification of problems is necessary. No man is without a weakness. The ability to accurately determine what our weakness are is crucial and is the fastest way to achieve success, because the barriers created by our weaknesses would be taken off our path by identifying them.

Motivational speakers commonly say, "There is nothing as powerful as a changed mind." This phrase is a comfort when we need to make radical changes to ensure that our goals are achieved. Pain is all in the brain. If our brain cells cannot process pain, we would invariably feel no pain. Moments where pain is felt are times should be treated as periods of self-reflection both for worker and individual. Organizations should produce a work climate that prompts workers to share their mistakes so they could be analyzed objectively to prevent future occurrences of the same issue.

There should be a limit between what is acceptable and what will not be acceptable. For example, anyone can walk into any super mart, hassle the cashier, and go off with the money and any item they feel is beneficial to them. If there are no laws governing the USA, the absence of what is allowed and what is not allowed would ultimately result in chaos. But with the existence of laws, such behaviors are not tolerated and when they do occur, there is a laid-out punishment for offenders.

The same thing applies to the organization. The fact that an open culture exists does not mean that every mistake would be tolerated and accepted. Workers should know what is accepted and what is not accepted to help them guide their conduct.

## CHAPTER 4

## GET AND STAY IN SYNC

Have you been to an opera before? If you have, I am sure you would definitely understand the importance of synchronization. If you have not, don't worry you would still understand where we are going in this chapter.

Alignment in an organization is as important as taking steps toward fulfilling your goals in the life principle section of this book. Believing that papering or avoiding disagreement is the best way to preserve peace is the wrong approach to achieving organization success. Rather, "thoughtful disagreement which is the process of having a quality back-and-forth discussion in an open-minded and assertive" manner is the singular most important aspect of achieving synchronization in the work place.

Peace is not the absence of conflict but the ability to handle them when they arise in such a way they do not spill over and begin to affect everyone. Meaningful relationships are not free of conflict, rather they are made up of continuous break-ups and make-ups. The key to attaining sync is to practice an organization culture that runs on meritocracy, in which disagreements are not suppressed but are used as a learning process for all. The same way we prioritize our choices should be the same way we separate disagreements, because not every complaint or disagreement leads to improvement of the organization.

In Life Principles, Mr. Dalio stated that open-mindedness is important in achieving success. Even here, the ability to simultaneously be open-minded and assertive is not common because typically we are inclined to be assertive rather than being open-minded. However, both skills need to be practiced and thought to improve the decision-making process. The first noticeable skill achieved from practicing assertiveness and being open-minded is the ability to distinguish between close-minded and open-minded people. After they have been identified, time should be spent on associating with open-minded people because interactions with close-minded people would yield no benefit.

Note: synchronization is a two-way street. Miscommunication will always happen but like every situation, it is important to learn from them. Asking questions and making suggestion are not the same thing. It is important that we ask open-minded questions and make suggestions when and where necessary to accelerate the success story both in our work and personal life.

Work place meetings are constantly organized, but in order to break the norm of having poor meetings in terms of their take-home knowledge make it clear the moment the meeting starts that you are in charge of the modus-operandis (that is the method of operation) of the meeting. Make the priority of the meeting known to everyone in attendance as this would forestall against future inappropriate behavior.

When handling an issue, such matters should be dealt with in levels rather than approaching the issue from all sides. If you notice that people are becoming highly emotional and disturbed by a particular issue, logic should be applied in analyzing the conversation after the analysis. Responsibility should be shared by all members of the meeting and the convener should ensure the main purpose of their gathering is completed in order to achieve synchronization. Alignment should be cherished when attained. If all parties involved are not able to come to a progressive point of synchronization, the value of the individual is compared with their general contribution to the organization to determine if it is advisable to keep them on your payroll or let them go.

## CHAPTER 5

## BELIEVABILITY WEIGHT YOUR DECISION-MAKING

In an organization where power is decentralized, decision-making is brought down to the lower-tier, while in a centralized organization only top officials are privileged to make decisions. The best decisions are made in meritocracy with believability-weighted decision-making. Having a merit hierarchy goes with idea meritocracy because in every group, one person is more knowledgeable on the topic of discussion than other members of the group thus increasing their believability level.

Do you know that not ever successful soccer coach was a great soccer player? The same thing applies to the organization. A person might be gifted in giving out instructions about a particular event without being able to carry out that event, if progress is to be maintained such person's words should not be treated with levity.

Open-mindedness is evident in our humility to genuinely understand another person's point of view on an issue. To succeed, do not just listen to believable people who share the same train of thought with you on all issues, rather, seek believable people who are in opposition with your line of action as this would help gain insight in the topic of focus. Believable people can be identified in different ways, including someone who has a possible explanation on the cause-effect relationship on the topic of discussion, someone who has a track record of successful accomplishments in the topic of discussion, someone who has understudied the topic of discussion for an extended period of time, etc. In attaining success, inexperienced people who have great thinking should be listened to because they might produce fresh and innovative ways of handling the issue the experienced person might be blind to.

In an organizational setting it is important to describe your role and that of all people involved because role description and understanding would help reducing ambiguity and confusion carrying out actions within the organization. It is one thing to get an answer to a question but more importantly is the fact you should create time to understand how these answers are arrived at. This probing into answers should not be carried out by everyone because it would lead to time wasting.

Have you imagined how stressful it can get when an organization's culture gives room for disagreements? Even when disagreements are not welcomed they constitute a nuisance in work place relationships since they are allowed.

The following steps should be followed to keep them in check: know when it is time to stop arguing and reach a consensus, use believability weighting as a tool to draw conclusions faster but they should not entirely substitute the decision-making process, choose the more experienced people wisely when handling disagreements because this would save you time, carefully compare your opinion with that of the crowd before proceeding to make judgement on any disagreements.

With these processes, the job of disagreeing in a productive and effective manner can be achieved. No one should be considered as inferior to another, thus communication within the organization should be aimed at getting the best answers from the most believable people. Communication should be carrying everyone along, even when the more believable people are saddled with the responsibility of making decisions. Communication should not always translate to selecting or making judgements, rather sometimes just getting everyone in sync would suffice as adequate communication.

## CHAPTER 6

## RECOGNIZE HOW TO GET BEYOND DISAGREEMENTS

Consistency is required to maintain integrity in every society and the work place is not any different. A common quote among the younger generation: "Rules are meant to be broken."

This phrase is essentially wrong in the work place because to maintain a high level of idea meritocracy, sincerity, honesty and rules must be applied to all and only modified when the whole body realizes there is a need for such modifications, and irrespective of your rank in the organization, the same rules should be binding on all.

Free communication is essential for upward movement in any business because it gives the employee the chance to call each other out when they make a wrong move or could carry out a task in a more productive way. In order to prevent chaos, decision-making should be streamlined to a selected few as this would ensure accountability across all levels.

One prominent way to get beyond disagreements is to handle them head on. Humans are wired to avoid conflict and confrontation but that would only work against the growth of an organization in the long run. If disagreements come up concerning any idea or personnel, it is important that such disagreements focus on a broad context of the organization's goals rather than a streamlined concept.

Pursuing the group goal is fundamental because every individual would have their own goal but when there is an alignment, all energy is focused toward attaining the same thing. Disagreements are welcomed because they provide opportunities for growth but another important factor is the ability to function even when your point of view is not the desired solution to a disagreement. Policies can be made to help members of an organization view situations from a higher level outside themselves. This is one way to help everyone get beyond disagreements that arise.

The hallmark of any successful business is the ability to adapt to changing times. In an event where there is conflict between the laid-out principles of the organization and current events or occurrences in the organization, the principles should be put on hold. For example, if trade secrets of an organization are made known to the general public, an organization can reduce information flow to only 'need-to-know' basis to protect the group.

Finally, irrespective of your position in the organization's hierarchy, principles must be respected and upheld by all or the organization will fail.

# TO GET THE PEOPLE RIGHT...

## CHAPTER 7

## REMEMBER THAT THE WHO IS MORE IMPORTANT THAN THE WHAT

Culture and people have a mutually beneficial relationship. One would not be totally complete without the existence of the other. Every culture attracts a certain kind of people. Billionaire Steve Jobs said once that Apple's success is partly hinged on the great extent to which the company goes to hire the right kind of people.

In every successful endeavor in life, it is more important to get the right people handling such duties than getting the duties right.

Picking the right individuals to perform a task is the foundation for success in every great institution. Picking the right person to carry out a task should not exclude you as the head of the organization. Senior managers should be able to differentiate between a goal and tasks as this is key in hiring right because hiring is a delicate process that involves the ability to distinguish between candidates to fit into each role.

Most successful men and women have a high internal focus of control. That is, when there is an error or mistake committed, they look inwardly to find the cause of the problem rather than blame other people. When selecting people to file a position, final nominees should be those who have their incentives and responsibilities aligned as this would help them in owning up to the consequences of their actions. This helps in improving accountability in the organization.

Big organizations are not built by their names but are built by the decisions made by their work force and leaders. Most people consider the power that is wielded by the mention of an organization but forget the people that helped build that power.

In order, to ensure there is continuous growth, the builders of every organization should not be forgotten. In fact, they should be rewarded for their immense contribution to the organization's success. This reward would help in cementing their loyalty to the organization and also motivate them to work harder.

# CHAPTER 8

## HIRE RIGHT, BECAUSE THE PENALTIES FOR HIRING WRONG ARE HUGE

In manufacturing, you hire people only after the creation of the design not before. The same goes for hiring. The nature of the job determines who is hired by the organization.

The first rule in hiring is to match the skill-set of those hired with the job description. Each new employee should have character, common sense, and creativity. This would improve the adaptability nature of the person hired. Hiring should be done using a tested system, not subjectively, as this would improve the type of individual's recruited. It is advisable to not use one's power to hire, rather each prospective employee should be hired through the right channel to prevent undermining the meritocracy policy.

People have different personalities, which they bring to the work place. It is important that in recruiting new members of the organization, each personality type should be understood to aid in hiring the right person to fit into particular roles. A special team of recruiters who can view people objectively irrespective of their own personality, should be used as this would reduce bias in hiring.

Recruiting should not just be based on academic qualifications, because school environment is different from the work environment and it is essential that recruiters keep that fact in mind. References should be explored in recruiting. They could be previous bosses, colleagues, or subordinates. Never assume that an individual would excel at a task in your organization because they have excelled elsewhere. The organization should be viewed as a professional sports team, where each member's success is required for the general success of the organization.

Just like when purchasing a tool, the functionality and durability are considered before purchase is made; same principles should be considered. New personnel should not just be people with great answers but also people with great questions as this would show their ability to be loyal in the long run.

This fact is key because they would always provide a different angle to handling any issues that arise along the way.

Compensation should not just be made on job title alone but on the person carrying out the job. The compensation should provide stability and opportunity as these two are essential in motivating employees. Generosity is more important than monetary value. Generosity could be in kind or monetary; which helps people realize they are valued and appreciated. Great people are hard to find, once identified it is essential to work toward keeping them.

## CHAPTER 9

## CONSTANTLY TRAIN, TEST, EVALUATE, AND SORT PEOPLE.

Learning is mandatory for evolution; this evolution is needed to remain relevant in what ever field of life you find yourself. Employers and employees are not exempt from this process. Excelling it is important to understand your strengths and weaknesses then work toward making the best out of them. Learning is not only found in books and seminars. Practical sessions should be conducted to improve overall knowledge.

In speaking the truth at all times, feelings are bound to be hurt but this should not stop the truth from being said. In the end, it is important to be accurate and kind in evaluating the performance of workers and criticize constructively rather than just criticize. Compliments should be given out as a boost to the morale of all.

Evaluation is as important as training. Every evaluation conducted reveals valuable information on the performance of each individual. Evaluations can be done with the use of standardized instruments. After the evaluation it is important to inform personnel about their performance level. It is also easier to sound emotion-free and honest when there is data to back up the conclusion arrived at after evaluation and makes it easier to forge a future line of action.

Metrics for evaluating performance should be easy to understand by all. This metric should also provide opportunity for each person to monitor their own performance. Reviews should be conducted based on a whole picture approach rather than a streamlined approach. An evaluation should be done not just based on results but on the process through which the results are received.

In organizations, evaluations usually occurs in one direction. In other to convince the manager of transparency in the evaluation process, it is important to explain the reason for each evaluation in detail. Frank conversations should be encouraged as they make it easier to discuss weaknesses and give room for change and improvement.

Talent and skill acquisition are prerequisites to good functioning. If any personnel is not functioning as expected, it is important to get to the root cause of the poor performance and determine if it is a problem in skill acquisition or innate abilities. If a person is lacking in skills, training can easily be conducted to improve their skills but in a scenario where talent is the issue, letting go of such individual could be beneficial.

In running an effective organization, objectivity is required in most cases to achieve the right results. Every manager must be willing to let slacking employees go, irrespective of their personal attachment because keeping such people would only result in reducing the organization's productivity. The same rigor should be used to evaluate both existing and new staff to ensure that everyone continues functioning at the organization's required level of success.

# TO BUILD AND EVOLVE YOUR MACHINE...

## CHAPTER 10

### MANAGE AS SOMEONE OPERATING A MACHINE TO ACHIEVE A GOAL

According to Mr. Dalio every good organization should be likened to a machine because it would involve designing (people) and executing designs through actions. Do not forget the goal of the organization as a result of small victories. Attention should also be paid to high priority cases to maximize all opportunities.

The goal at every point in an organization should be the attainment of excellence. Managers should take caution in paying attention to individual tasks because they would eventually become worn out if there is no delegation of duties.

Every organization will continue to be faced with different cases. These cases should be handled in a way that provides opportunity to test and train workers. Organizational principles should lead to the creation of policies to guide the everyday making of decisions about cases to be handled. There is always room to make exceptions but this should not be a regular occurrence as it could weaken the principles guiding the organization.

Exceptional managers can be likened to music conductors in an orchestra. They do not handle every individual activity but they are in charge of harmonizing everyone's individual role to attain excellence. Management should not be done from a higher ground rather the manager should act as a director who delegates duties to each staff, and instructs them on what is expected of them, then gives them the space to operate and execute the plans laid out for them. This description is the difference between managing, micro-managing, and not managing at all.

Handling humans can be tricky yet easy to achieve. Every manager should have a full profile on each employee. Creating a personal rapport with the employee would also give the manager opportunity to know them better and make it easier for him to delegate duties to the right personnel and know how much confidence he can have about their ability to perform.

Ambiguity only breads confusion, so the manager should clearly assign duties to avoid confusion and make it easy for him or her to trace "job slips" when they occur. Every manager needs to stay on top of every task. One way of achieving this act is to relate to employees rather than act as an authoritarian. This would enable managers to detect a problem before it occurs. Every manager should improve their listening skills for non-verbal communication cues and train their ears to listen.

Managers should make every staff feel responsible for the organization and handle it as if it were their own. Based on ranking, each employee should be treated with the respect they deserve. As a manager, it is possible to occasionally allow staff to see some weakness in you; makes it easier for them to realize you are also human, but don't worry, not everyone will like you, which is normal. Finally, every employee should be held accountable. As the manager, not being exempted because this is the true way to practice radical transparency and meritocracy.

# CHAPTER 11

## PERCEIVE AND DON'T TOLERATE PROBLEMS

The road to success is not smooth and problem-free. In fact, encountering problems are inevitable. To be successful you must be able to see problems and not tolerate them. Problems should be viewed as growth time because when viewing them from a level of higher thinking. For a lot of people, they prefer the comfort of success than the pains of problems but like the popular quote: "No pain, no gain."

Mr. Dalio provided three principles to help guide the process of perceiving and handling problems: "If you're not worried, you need to worry, and if you're worried, you don't need to worry." This principle is rooted in the fact that worrying about what might go wrong would increase your alertness and most likely help you in detecting problems quickly; however, the other part explains that in being too relaxed might make it difficult to detect a problem early enough and can even lead to mistakes because of the levity with which duties are handled.

As a manager, be the central overseer of all creations as this would enable you detect early on what plans or decisions are not good for the organization. Be proactive in identifying problems. People can even be assigned to carry out those actions. Beware of the psychological phenomenon called, "group thinking," because the fact that everyone accepts it doesn't make it the right decision. The perspective of all employees, especially those closer to a job, should be heard.

As a manager, being specific about the root cause of a problem makes it easier to create a solution. If the problem is caused by a staff member, do not mask it as a group problem rather let that individual know their role in the problem. Finally, do not be afraid to fix problems. Get the right people to handle the situation and create a plan to avoid such issues in the future.

## CHAPTER 12

## DIAGNOSE PROBLEMS TO GET AT THEIR ROOT CAUSES

In chapter 11 we talked about identifying the root cause of a problem as an easy way to solve any problem. The most common mistakes made by managers is not identifying the root cause of a problem. Usually after diagnosis, they just move on to fix the issue without probing to confirm if that is the root cause of their problem. Another, prominent issue is not learning from previous mistakes made. This would enable them to view problems from the bigger picture rather than a localized occurrence.

To ensure that diagnosis yields the right result, it is important to diagnose correctly. Questions such as:

- "Is the outcome good or bad?"
- "Who is responsible for the outcome?"
- "If the outcome is bad, is the responsible party incapable and/or is the design bad?"

With these questions in mind, it is easy to use the big picture approach. Do not streamline yourself to these questions alone. Depending on your organization and the nature of the problem, you can vary your questions.

When the nature of the problem outcome is defined, it is important to verify if the problem is in the organizational design or in a person and to understand why events did not pan out as expected. This would enable you to know the appropriate next step or steps. Always remember, every diagnosis should produce results.

When the root cause of a problem is identified, as a manager you should ensure the problem is not a pattern of events. If the root cause is a pattern, the other parts of it should be handled alongside the problem. If the problem is with an individual, it should be determined if the issue is a capacity or capability problem. In summary, diagnose problems and get to the root cause:

Step 1: List the problems.
Step 2: Identify the root causes.

Step 3: Create a plan.

Step 4: Execute the plan.

## CHAPTER 13

## DESIGN IMPROVEMENTS TO YOUR MACHINE TO GET AROUND YOUR PROBLEMS

After diagnosis is complete and successful the next step is to create a solution to the problem discovered. It is one thing to have guiding principles and it is a different situation to ensure they are continually practiced.

Every manager should create a systematic way of implementing principles that guide the organization. Every good plan should be transitional like a movie script. The plans should be easy to visualize because it is easy to carry the workforce along when they have a visual of what is expected of them.

Remember in second- and third-order consequences discussed in the part II of this book, they should be analyzed in improving the design and work plans of your organization. Your organization design should always factor in that humans are imperfect and as such are liable to make mistakes. Creating good work design is an iterative process that involves continuous changing, restructuring, testing, and re-designing. To run a successful large organization, "cleansing storms" should be welcomed because they remove the unproductive portion to provide room for the productive arms to flourish.

Goals are symbolic to the larger picture while tasks are symbolic to just a little portion of the larger picture. Organizations should be built around goals not tasks to ensure longevity. Organizations should be built from top down; the organization is not found in the building but rather in the people that make-up the building and as such its foundation is the executives and managers. There must be strong oversight with each person being accountable to someone. It is the duty of the managers to ensure each head of a unit possesses the necessary skills to head such unit and understand their duties as unit heads. As managers, every team should be comprised of members with different abilities to aid working together.

Do not build the organization to fit people. A manager's job should not be designed to fit personnel, rather people with the capability to deliver such jobs should be hired. Jobs should be designed based on the overall goal of the organization. This is the way great industries have continued to remain relevant.

In creating organizational designs, the resources available for use should be considered. Some organizations might have so much capital that they could have their own structure from the on-set while others would not have the capital to own their building in the beginning.

In some cases, it is okay to ration resources between different units but each unit should be as self-sufficient as possible. Every manager should create a work design that would allow for transition of power and continuity with or without them. This would include more than just creating a system that would be enacted when you step down as manager but would include selection, training, and governing of new leaders.

In making mission-critical decisions, it is essential you assign at least two individuals to carry out such task as this would aid in double-doing rather than double-checking, which would cost more time and resources to be spent in some cases. Note: in fixing organizational problems, it is okay to use consultants but most importantly watch out for consultant addiction. In some cases it is more economical to train your own personnel than to continue hiring outside help.

As a manager, it is important you think of the bigger picture and smaller picture together. Keep your strategic vision in place while making appropriate changes as new situations arise. Trust everyone but investigate them. Either way, this would enable you have a solid base for your trust.

## CHAPTER 14

### DO WHAT YOU SET OUT TO DO

If you love your job there is an inner joy that is evident in all that you do. Every organization should be geared toward goals that excite them. If you are thrilled by the goals and tasks assigned to you, you will be willing to go the extra mile to achieve them even if those extra steps are not convenient. As a manger, you would require well organized plans and consistency to motivate your staff. These steps could be emotionally or intellectually done.

Timing can be tricky but as a manager it is important that you think before acting. The time spent on creating a solid plan should not be considered as a waste. When people with problems arise, try to discover the most innovative and clear-cut way to solve the problem. Some people tend to devote a lot of time to solving one issue while others would accomplish the same task in a relatively shorter period of time. What makes the difference? Creativity, character, and wisdom are the difference.

Winston Churchill was absolutely right when he said, "Success consists of going from failure to failure without loss of enthusiasm." Life is a like day and night, no matter how long one lasts the other would eventually show up; but like how inventions has created very bright lights to brighten our nights the same can be done in life's night.

Check list can be used to ensure that each person meets their expected duties and deadlines. It is important we do not confuse a check list with responsibilities. Check list is made up of chores, while our responsibilities could include a whole lot more.

A saying goes: "You cannot cheat nature." The human body requires rest to function adequately. In fact, some researchers have shown through research that productivity level drops with increased sleep deprivation or absence of rest. Every organization as such should provide room for rest and rejuvenation because in the long run, such times would be beneficial to the organization. And at last, when victory is attained do not forget to celebrate.

## CHAPTER 15

## USE TOOLS AND PROTOCOLS TO SHAPE HOW WORK IS DONE

Words alone cannot suffice. Remember, if wishes were horses, all men could ride them. Every organizational principle should be embedded in the designs and modus-operandis of the organization. This is valuable to run an idea meritocracy system.

In running an organization, managers should be thoroughly scrutinized using an evidence-based process to maintain objectivity. Behavior cannot be changed without practice. To ensure real behavioral change practice is the key. In this age and time, technology has helped in greatly improving the learning process.

Learning can be done through other means apart from reading. Learning can be executed through visuals, audio, simulations, or in most cases multimedia mediums. Today, data is considered as the next big thing. Enormous amounts of data can be collected and analyzed to help provide well-cut guideline on how to handle a situation

As a manager, it is your duty to create and foster a work environment that gives room for confidence and fairness by imbedding your organization principles in your work protocol.

Workers should be given the freedom to air their own opinion of a good decision-making process. This would help prevent feeling of unfairness when decisions are arrived at using their proposed ideas.

## CHAPTER 16

## AND FOR HEAVEN'S SAKE, DON'T OVERLOOK GOVERNANCE!

Governing is the process of taking charge of a group of people, where by one or more individuals are placed as the central authorities. To be successful, all organizations must have checks and balances. With checks, meaning someone to report to, and balance to decentralize power.

In idea meritocracy, decisions cannot be made based on merits alone. There are times when the management and employees might not have the same ideology on an issue. Such disagreements should be handled in a way that would produce the best result rather than what is wanted by all. Ensure that no one is so powerful they cannot be replaced because this would undermine the existing rule of law and become a thorny situation to handle.

At all times, loyalty should be directed toward the organization rather than head of units or supervisors as this would help prevent conflicts when tough decisions are made. As managers, supervision direction should be clear and easily understood by all. Whoever is saddled with the duty of carrying out assessments, should be one with no conflict of interest and must be trustworthy enough to handle information presented before him or her.

Always remember that in idea meritocracy, two heads are better than one. Dependence on a single person creates opportunity for checks and balance of the organization to be eroded, and finally with all these ideas in place great partnerships should be formed with other organization to help improve the process of climbing to success.

# CONCLUSION

This book was written to pass on Mr. Dalio's success principles to anyone interested in learning how he was able to grow a billion-dollar company from scratch.

*"I, of course, hope that they will help you visualize your own audacious goals, navigate through your painful mistakes, have quality reflections, and come up with good principles of your own that you will systematically follow to produce outcomes that vastly exceed your expectations. I hope that they will help you do these things both individually and when working with others. And, since your journey and evolution will certainly be a struggle, I hope that these principles will help you struggle and evolve well. Perhaps they will even inspire you and others to put your principles in writing and collectively figure out what's best in an idea-meritocratic way. If I could tilt the world even one degree more in that direction, that would thrill me." Mr. Ray Dalio.*